WHISPERS OF A VAGABOND

MONISHKA

Dedicated to the vagabonds

who carried the agony to their graves.

When souls' bleeds!

It goes like –

The agony of heart,

spilled on a paper,

with the eternal torment,

of a vagabond.

CONTENTS

SHIP

TRAUMATIZED

LOVE

WHY?

MY DEATHBED

LOST

HUMANS

DEATH

YOUNG SOUL

ABANDONED

UNTOLD

Foreword

In the quiet spaces between words, poetry holds the power to illuminate the human experience like no other art form. As I leaf through the pages of "Whispers of A Vagabond", I am struck by the lyrical beauty and profound insights that grace each poem. Monishka has crafted a collection that transcends mere verses, offering readers a profound journey through the landscapes of emotion, memory and reflection. With a keen eye for detail and a deft touch with language. Monishka invites us to explore the complexities of love, the rhythms of nature and the depths of the human soul.

Through these poems, we encounter moments of tenderness, resilience and wonder. Each poem is a testament to the author's sensitivity to the nuances of life and their ability to distil universal truths into poignant verses. Whether capturing the fleeting beauty of a sunset or delving into the intricacies of the personal identity, approaches each subject with grace and insight.

As you delve into this collection, prepared to be moved and inspired. These poems are not merely reflections of one individual's experience but mirrors

Preface

Welcome to "Whispers of A Vagabond". In this anthology of poems, I invite you to explore a journey through emotions, experiences and reflections that have shaped my perspective on life and the world around us.

Poetry, for me, has always been a means of expressing the ineffable, capturing fleeting moments and distilling complex feelings into words. Each poem in this collection is a snapshot of a moment in time - a moment of joy, sorrow, contemplation or revelation. As you read through these pages, you may encounter themes of love and loss, nature and nostalgia, identity and introspection. These poems are not just my own experiences but also a reflection of universal human emotions and aspirations.

I have drawn inspirations from various sources - personal encounters, nature's beauty, philosophical musings and profound stories of everyday life. Each poem is a testament to the power of language and the ability of words to evoke emotions and provoke thoughts. I hope these poems resonate with you in some way, offering moments of solace, inspiration or simply a quiet reflection.

Poetry has a unique way of connecting us across time and space, and I am grateful for the opportunity to share this collection with you.

Thank you for embarking on this poetic journey with me. May these verses inspire you to see the world with new eyes and to find beauty in the ordinary.

Monishka

Acknowledgement

I am deeply grateful to everyone who contributed to the completion of this book. Your support and encouragement have been invaluable.

First and foremost, I want to thank my teachers whose keen insights and meticulous attention to details greatly improved the clarity and coherence of this collection.

I am indebted to my friends who provided me with crucial insights that shaped the content of chapters. A special thanks to my mother for the unwavering support and encouragement throughout the writing process. Your belief in this project kept me motivated during challenging times.

I extend my appreciation to my family for their patience, understanding, and unwavering belief in me.

Your love and encouragement sustained me through this journey.

Lastly, I want to acknowledge the reviewers whose constructive feedback helped me refine this work.

Thank you for embarking on this journey with me. May these verses accompany you like old friends, offering companionship and illumination along the way.
With warmth and gratitude,
Monishka

About The Author

Born in Gujarat on 14-08-2007. Monishka started her poetic journey at a tender age of 14. Her work explores themes of emotions and experiences. She currently resides in Jaipur and finds inspiration in the scenic beauty and culture of this city.

Through this book, she brings her ideas to life and hope to connect with readers. While writing this piece of art, the overwhelming emotions came like a peaceful wind in the season of spring.

Do they speak?

If yes, then my goes like;

The agony of my heart,

*Flooded down on my cheeks in the
form of water.*

*But for how long, it can leave my
eyes red?*

Forever!

The torment of those red veins,

*I got for the first time when
I was completely, broken.*

You will bear the pain of life,
You will keep searching for peace of heart.

When wound of heart will torture you,
then you will remember only one person.

Monishka

What is a gathering without you in it?
What is an evening without you?
And...
What is that heart? Which is
not attached to you!

Stab me with that cold knife,
It still won't be colder than your eyes.
Keep it there a while,
Though knowing you,
You'd probably twist it left or right.

Chop me inside out,
Bleed me dry,
Whatever it takes,

To have you by my side.

Monishka

SWIMMERS

laying, thinking,
the last night!
in this world of swimmers,
do I'll be able to swim or just
sink?
in the chaotic ocean,
to find a home for my soul,
today, someday or never!
the whispers of breeze,
the susurration of waves,
the sound of nature, tranquillity! but
the next,
I wish I was just a grave,
or just sprinkle of ash in the next
wave.
this ocean is a silent cave,
peaceful sleep is ever there,
beneath the dark blue waves!

BEAUTY

in the tapestry of life,
your presence shines bright.
a vision of beauty in morning's soft light.
with each graceful move, you cast a spell.
a melody of love, in which I dwell.
your essence, a masterpiece beyond
compares.
a garden of roses, tender and rare.
in your eyes, I find a true life.
a captivating allure, like morning dew.
so here I lay, my heart humbly,
in you I've found my muse,
a timeless beauty,
I'll forever choose you.

MOTHER

looking in the mirror of world,
how people change,
but constant defines her.
knotting the tie of love and compassion;
today and forever.
keeping away the pall of phony
and covering up all with generosity.
God is you and not any other marble art.

HOME

four walls echo memories
curtains swung with happy breeze
sun that falls upon the table
words which provided strength
pigeons who saw watery eyes
happiness and sorrows were briefed
works were collaborated
laughter that lips hold
letters were read with patience
atlas; who I was
debates remained undebated
nicknames which were named forever
candy which holds the sweetness
stories written for eternity in hearts
hugs that pall peace
taught prayers have powers
a sigh of understanding
the months spent in joy
-with the person who loved!

Monishka

YOUR GRAVE

you destroyed me,
when you closed your eyes.
the immortal peace was yours,
the immortal pain was mine.
not a second passed,
and you disappeared like
nowhere.
in the evening,
when the sun paints the sky in
west.
I'd stand alone, with your
memories in my eyes.
the tears poured out like rain and
your absence turned it into a
storm.
we are still those,
what we were, yesterday.
beneath the sky and the stars,
you rest with my heart.
the dead flowers holding in my hands,
I uttered a silent,
goodbye!

YOUNG, DUMB, BROKE

don't cry too much,
it shall pass,
consoling that broken heart,
every golden hour.
day or night,
i loved them twice.
we're no longer the souls; we
met few weeks back. there's
no forever meant to be,
every strong heart breaks.
young souls with broken
heart.
I heard an old man - yesternight declaring,
"we're too young to be broken."

YOU

you say,
you defile everything you touch
but you purify my rotten soul.
you're the ease to my ripped agony
heart.
the ointment on my blood flowing wound,
you're the daylight to a wither
flower.
the moon glade to the parched,
river flowing behind the hills.
you're the aroma to my insipidity,
the filament of an aged bulb,
you're the firefly of my grey life,
the serendipity of my uncharted life,
you're the serene to my turbulent mind,
you're the shore of a boundless sea,
the ocean of my raindrops,
the dusk for every dawn,
you're the famous story of my gathering,
you're the divine of the devil mankind,
you're the life to a corpse,
you're an abode forever to a
parasite.

CHILD

the cherished love,
the child yearned for.
the soft cotton heart,
with lumpy scars.
the loquacious her,
paused being a
taciturn.
the words were cruel,
like fuel on the fire.
planted a barbed wire,
around my throat.
the agony of my heart,
ripped off the eyes
apart.
the child not weep for opulent things
anymore,
but *for a haven*.
where the agony of her heart,
takes the permanent departure.

Monishka

RAIN

in the quiet solitude night,
the clouds were crying
heavily, the trees were
shaking terribly.
the night owl with watery lashes,
losing on life.
the vibrations of hate,
keeping her in pain.
rain in heart, rain on roof.
the memories disappeared
under the grey,
whispers the sun rays.
with every drop it tells a story,
which is never going to regain.
the cold breeze takes the love away,
a symphony of nature's tears,
a gentle stroke,
rain, a hope,
in every droplet it spoke.

THE CHAOS

in the buzz of this chaotic mess,
my eyes still wander for you.
the unleashed love we made in
silence,
departed us with cacophony.
your eyes were coffee beans;
rich and dark.
the intimacy of holding hands,
abandoned in grace.
the canvas we painted together,
is now a beautiful painting for every
passerby.
our love vanished like water,
in no time and place.
you will be always my song,
remembered and euphonious.
you will be always my poetry,
beautifully written and composed.
but none of this celebration,
can bring us back together.
this sung world is always unsung without
you.
though you're gone from sight,
but by love we're always bound.

Monishka

WHAT IF?

people always say,
that calm down
"The moment"
everything will be good,
give some time.
but what if?
that moment I'm dying of pain.
what if?
that moment I just want to give up.
what if?
that moment I need someone.
what if?
that moment I'm drifting apart.
what if?
that moment I'm taking my last breath.
what if?
that moment I am going to rest forever.
what if?
that moment you lose me for forever?

LETTING GO!

I had thousands of tears,
when I whispered to let it go.
it's unbelievable for me,
to summarize that I did that.
the most selfless and painful
act, the art of letting go.
my eyes really anchor the pain of betrayal,
worthlessness and self-destruction
within me.
my heart still beats like it did the day we
met.
but the pain overlaps the unconditional
love.
you never taught me to unlove you,
you never taught me to live without you.
I still can't believe you did this to me,
why my life is shuffling?
why my eyes are draining?
why my hands are trembling?
tell me,
this is a nightmare;
it's not the end of us.

Monishka

APOCALYPSE

in the midst of summer,
your love bloom.
if love was just a seed,
you'd be each and every flower of my
garden.
those black eyes of yours,
could swallow me all.
if heartbeat was a language,
you'd be its love letter at dawn.
the moon always whispers,
your beauty.
yes, the stars are jealous.
our intimacy of holding hands,
tingling fingers,
 makes my soul warm.
my clothes just smell like you,
that I would never get off them.
they are all I could have now.
your love, my love,
apocalypse!

ARTISTS

darkness doesn't seem to be
forever.
the uncontrolled rage in every
soul,
which the innocence hides.
shakes out through eyes,
every drop speaks, the
cold truth, which they put
out of sight.
the rare art,
which only artists'
design.
the unexpressed
emotions,
the unspoken words,
beyond all limitations,
it's them with their designs.

SHIP

I'm breaking down,
like a sinking ship in the sea.
imagining, picturing, scripting!
the unleashed love, we created,
 on the spring days and the cosy
nights. i had it all and then most of
you, some and now none of you!
it's me with my love,
drowning in the sea…
the waves whispered,
that it's the time to
 let it go!

TRAUMATIZED

her soul is trembling by the voices in her
head,
the flood of water subsides in her eyes,
burning in the lake of fire,
lost the battles of life.
she gave up on smile,
is really this love she deprived?
a traumatized inner
child,
less on life,
day or night.
wished a tranquil pause -
from the chaos of life.

LOVE

oh, my beloved,
love can happen
endlessly.
gaining and losing,
is a part of love.
the matched desires,
the unmatched emotions.
before all the passion,
before all the pain.
I can be prodigal, with tears and blood.
an incomplete sentence,
which I wished to take a pause with a
comma, is now permanently ended with a
full stop.
let's go back to the second before we met.
we can now laugh that how,
we broke each other, until we make love
again.

WHY?

you're not mine,
but sometimes,
I wish you were.
when the world shattered
me,
you were the saviour,
you drew the best
memories.
but now we can't,
so, I'll write...
until my hand cramps,
until the tears start flowing,
until the cries of my heart are temporarily
silent.
I'll write until the urge to run to you,
has momentarily faded away.

Monishka

MY DEATHBED

I lay on my deathbed,
with the flowers,
I used to mention you.
deep beneath your shaking skin,
whispering my name.
as my body lies in an alone field of
flowers,
your tears watering the blooms.
thinking of the day,
we promised each other for forever!
but there's no existence of your beloved
now,
am I still your last hope to love?
I broke my first promise,
as usual I did all,
but with every smile you accepted them.
I want you to accept,
this last broken promise with a smile,
for the last time.

LOST

lost in the reverie,
a world so serene.
to be lost in lust of life,
with the crayons of mine.
living in the realms of dreams,
floating being known to this unknown
field.
a vagabond with melancholy soul,
stepped out of the tenebrosity.
delicate heart whispering about reminisces.
awful phrases of life,
tuned so high
with the prettiest scars,
of the *wildest child.*

Monishka

HUMANS

different creatures with indifferent emotions,
sometimes love, sometimes pain, sometimes
sympathy.
the addiction of love,
barbed with thorns.
longing for the endless possibilities,
from the unfeasible desires.
yesterday, today, tomorrow!
they never assumed themselves wrong.
maybe,
written perfectly in this imperfect ocean.
picturing themselves as the
creators,
towards the god of mankind.
bowing down in the chapel,
for the sins performed on this
land.
you, me and everyone,
are in the same loop of life.
it's us –
the most selfish creatures,
humans!

DEATH

maybe death is my muse,
it is fortunate,
hitting like an asteroid.
the lava rippling out of my eyes.
I clasp every death I've ever known, in my
palms holding a locket tight. echoes of pain
revolving inside out, for the eternal rest of
my soul.
I don't know where my soul will reside.
until then,
may he embrace me in his arms, and
welcomes me home safely.

Monishka

YOUNG SOUL

a soul so deep with thoughts untold, a heart
that's heavy with stories untold.
they yearn to speak to share their mind,
but words get trapped and silence they find. their
eyes reveal the depths inside,
a world of emotions they cannot hide.
but still they quiet their voice suppressed,
a million thoughts in their heart repressed.
in crowds they're lost in silence they're found,
their words unspoken;
their thoughts unbound.
they observe and listen with a careful ear, but their
own voice they rarely clear. perhaps they fear the
judgment of others,
or maybe they doubt their own discover.
but still,
they hold their thoughts inside,
and in the silence their heart does reside.
if only they knew the power of their voice, the
impact it could have the hearts they could rejoice.
but until then,
they'll stay quiet and still,
a soul with a lot to say, but unspoken will.

ABANDONED

in the midst of gloom,
you lend me your shoulder.
on the graveyard of my emotions,
you held my sensations.
in the flock of crows,
you were my pigeon.
in the thorn of roses,
you comforted me with tulip. the broken
strings of my heart, were stringed by
you with pearls.
the ink spilled out of my eyes, was
wiped by you.
you narrated my grey life,
with thousands of coloured verses.
you made me feel like a rainbow,
in the colourless ocean.
being this finest to my life.
I now, owe you a question;
why are you taking me to the graveyard of me
life every dawn, leaving me in the
middle of the scary mind of my
own.

Monishka

UNTOLD

your presence was a warm hug,
it's your absence which is hitting me like a cold
breeze.
my eyes are dry now;
as I poured an ocean out.
my heart still longs for you,
after all your betrayal.
for you, maybe, we are past memory,
for me, you are my present!
and so, i do love you.

we promised an eternity;
then why only my heart is sticked here.
you're everywhere but not here.
it's a lost love,
a memory that doesn't knocks your door anymore.
as you have faded me, away from you.
in everything, I search for you,
i look for you, I long for you.
you are not here,
your love is not here.
because you're gone,
leaving you here.

Whispers of a Vagabond